100

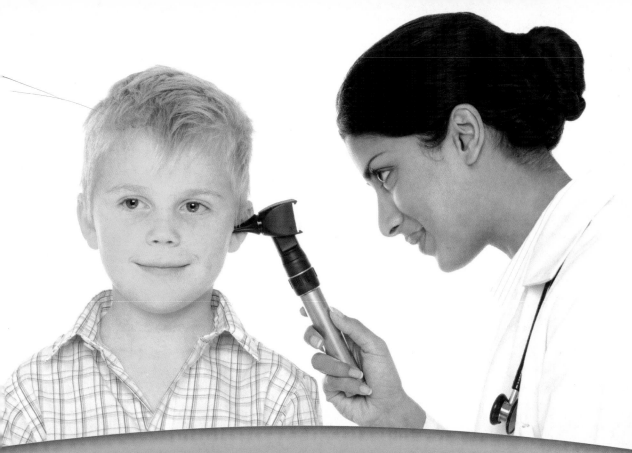

All About Your
EARS

Jenny Fretland VanVoorst
and Maria Koran

www.av2books.com

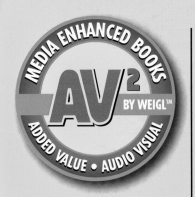

AV² provides enriched content that supplements and complements this book. Weigl's AV² books strive to create inspired learning and engage young minds in a total learning experience.

Your AV² Media Enhanced books come alive with...

Audio
Listen to sections of the book read aloud.

Key Words
Study vocabulary, and complete a matching word activity.

Video
Watch informative video clips.

Quizzes
Test your knowledge.

Go to **www.av2books.com**, and enter this book's unique code.

BOOK CODE

R756639

Embedded Weblinks
Gain additional information for research.

Slide Show
View images and captions, and prepare a presentation.

AV² by Weigl brings you media enhanced books that support active learning.

Try This!
Complete activities and hands-on experiments.

... and much, much more!

Published by AV² by Weigl
350 5th Avenue, 59th Floor
New York, NY 10118
Website: www.av2books.com

Library of Congress Cataloging-in-Publication Data

Names: Fretland VanVoorst, Jenny, 1972- author. | Koran, Maria, author.
Title: Ears / Jenny Fretland VanVoorst and Maria Koran.
Description: New York, NY : AV2 by Weigl, [2017] | Series: All about your...
  | Includes bibliographical references and index.
Identifiers: LCCN 2016034632 (print) | LCCN 2016035181 (ebook) | ISBN
  9781489651341 (hard cover : alk. paper) | ISBN 9781489651358 (soft cover :
  alk. paper) | ISBN 9781489651365 (Multi-user ebk.)
Subjects: LCSH: Ear--Juvenile literature. | Hearing--Juvenile literature.
Classification: LCC QP462.2 .F74 2017 (print) | LCC QP462.2 (ebook) | DDC
  612.8/5--dc23
LC record available at https://lccn.loc.gov/2016034632

Printed in the United States of America in Brainerd, Minnesota
1 2 3 4 5 6 7 8 9 0 20 19 18 17 16

082016
210716

Project Coordinator: Piper Whelan   Art Director: Terry Paulhus

Contents

Chapter 1
Listening to Your Ears

Our world is made up of sounds. Some sounds are soft and give us comfort. Other sounds are loud and warn us of danger. We would not hear these sounds without our ears. Ears are a part of the **auditory system**. This is the body system that helps us hear. The ears catch **sound waves** and turn them into messages the brain can understand.

Loud sounds can hurt our ears.

Sound waves go in your ear through the small holes on either side of your head.

Sound waves become the purr of a cat or the honk of a car horn. When you listen to music or your friend's funny story, your brain **decodes** sound waves. This is called hearing. Our ears are two of the most important parts of our body because they allow us to hear. Hearing is one of our most important senses. Being able to hear helps us speak and listen to others.

Look in the mirror. You have an ear on either side of your head. Earlobes are the fatty part at the bottom of your ears. Each ear helps you tell where sound waves are coming from. See how your ears are cup-shaped and face forward? They act like a funnel to trap and focus sound waves.

The part of your ear you can see is called the **outer ear**. The outer ear is only a small part of your ear. The parts that turn the sound waves into messages for your brain are on the inside.

Some ear parts help you keep your balance. In one part of your **inner ear**, fluid moves in tubes. The way the fluid moves around helps your brain understand the way your body is moving. The brain sends messages to the muscles to keep you from falling over. Without balance, you would not be able to ride a bike without training wheels.

Some people's earlobes connect to their head, while others are separated. Which do you have?

Cupping your hand behind your ear can help your ear to focus sound waves.

Chapter 2

How Ears Work

Follow the path a sound wave takes to your brain. Imagine your teacher has called your name. Your name comes out of her mouth as a sound wave. The wave travels through the air to your ear. The outer ear funnels the wave inside to the middle part of your ear. This part is called the **middle ear**. There, the sound wave travels through a narrow tube until it reaches the **eardrum**.

The eardrum acts like the top of a drum. When sound waves hit the eardrum, the eardrum **vibrates**. The vibrations move through three tiny bones in your middle ear.

The middle ear is smaller than a jelly bean.

The three bones in your middle ear are called the hammer, the anvil, and the stirrup. They are the tiniest bones in the human body. They make the sound waves bigger so you can hear them. The three bones move vibrations into the inner ear. Then, the vibrations enter a tube called the **cochlea**. The cochlea is filled with liquid.

The cochlea has tiny hairs inside. The vibrations move the liquid over the hairs. When the hairs move, they send a message to the brain. The brain decodes this message, and it becomes a sound. You know this sound as your name. You also know it was your teacher who spoke, and from what direction the sound came from.

Have you ever felt sick to your stomach while riding in a car? Motion sickness happens when your ears send messages to the brain that do not match the messages your other senses send.

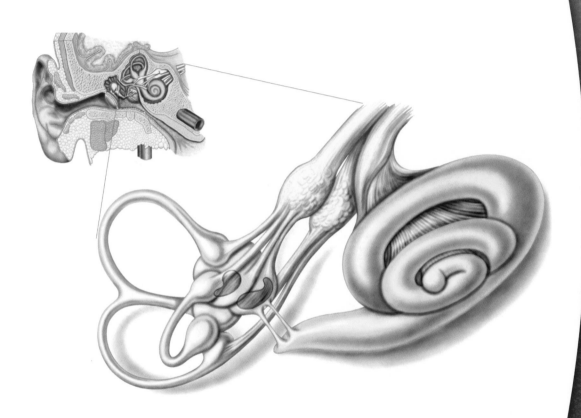

The cochlea is shaped like a snail shell, spiraling out from the center.

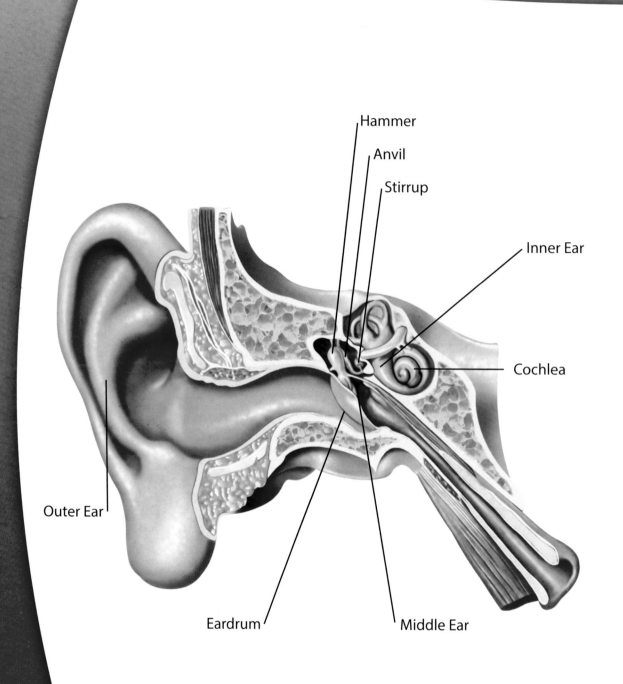

Hammer

Anvil

Stirrup

Inner Ear

Cochlea

Outer Ear

Eardrum

Middle Ear

Have you ever listened to a recording of your voice and thought it did not sound like you? When you speak, your outer ear catches the sound waves. The sound waves also travel directly through your head to reach your inner ear.

Your voice sounds deeper to you than it does to others because you hear sound waves from both parts of your ear. Record yourself talking to hear how you sound to others. When you listen to the recording, you will only hear the sound waves your outer ear picks up.

Chapter 3

When Ears Do Not Work

Our ears do a great job helping us listen to people and hear sounds. Unfortunately, ears do not always work as they should. Ear infections happen when **germs** get stuck in the different parts of the ear. Fluid can then get trapped in the middle ear. Your middle ear traps the fluid to try to help fight away the germs. All of the fluid makes your ears hurt, and it can make it hard to hear.

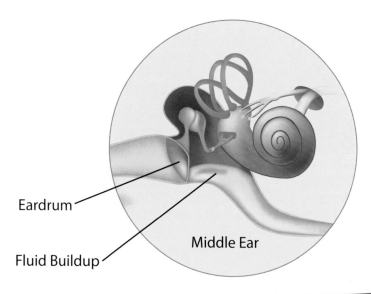

Eardrum

Middle Ear

Fluid Buildup

A doctor will look in your ears at each check-up.

Medicine can help fix most ear infections. People who get a lot of ear infections may need an operation. A doctor will put small tubes inside the ear to help drain the fluid.

As we get older, we can start to lose our hearing. The loud noises we hear can damage the inner ear. When sound waves travel across the hairs in the inner ear, they bend the hairs like grass bends in the wind. Over time, the hairs can stay bent. If the hairs are bent over, they cannot move to send a message to the brain. Hearing aids can help people of all ages hear more sounds.

The middle ear makes a sound 150 times louder to help decode the noise.

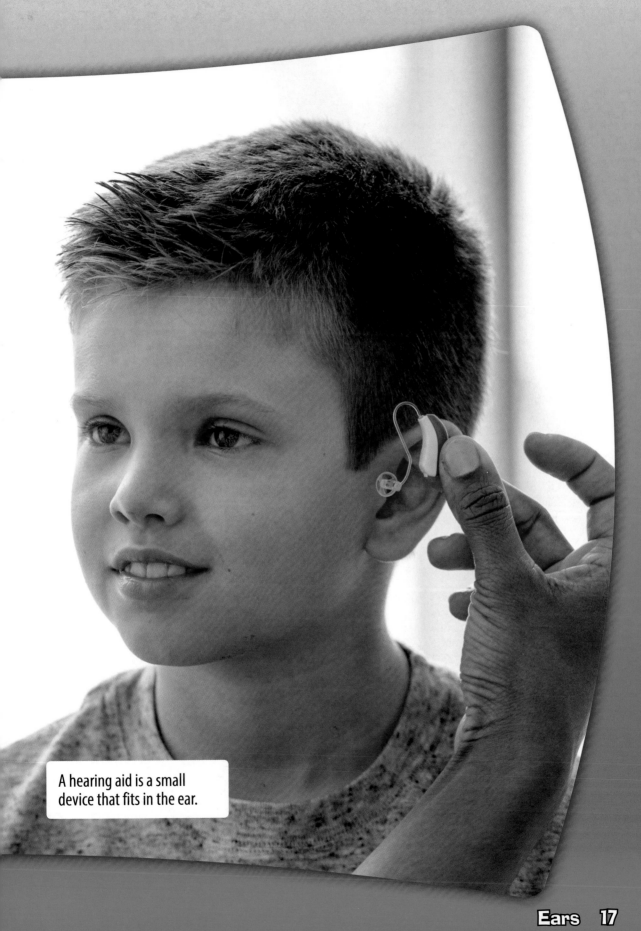

A hearing aid is a small device that fits in the ear.

Chapter 4
Taking Care of Your Ears

Ears can take care of themselves. One of the ways they do this is by making earwax. Earwax is made by **glands** in the outer ear. This sticky wax traps dust and other small particles before they get inside the ear.

Earwax has an important job to do. You do not need to remove it. The only thing that is safe to put in your ear is sound.

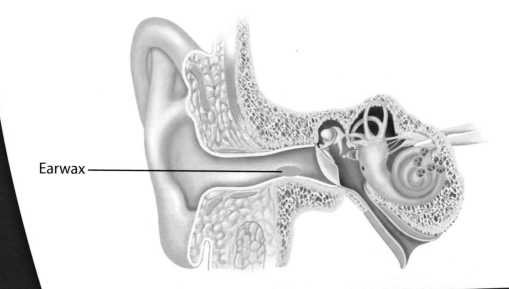

Earwax

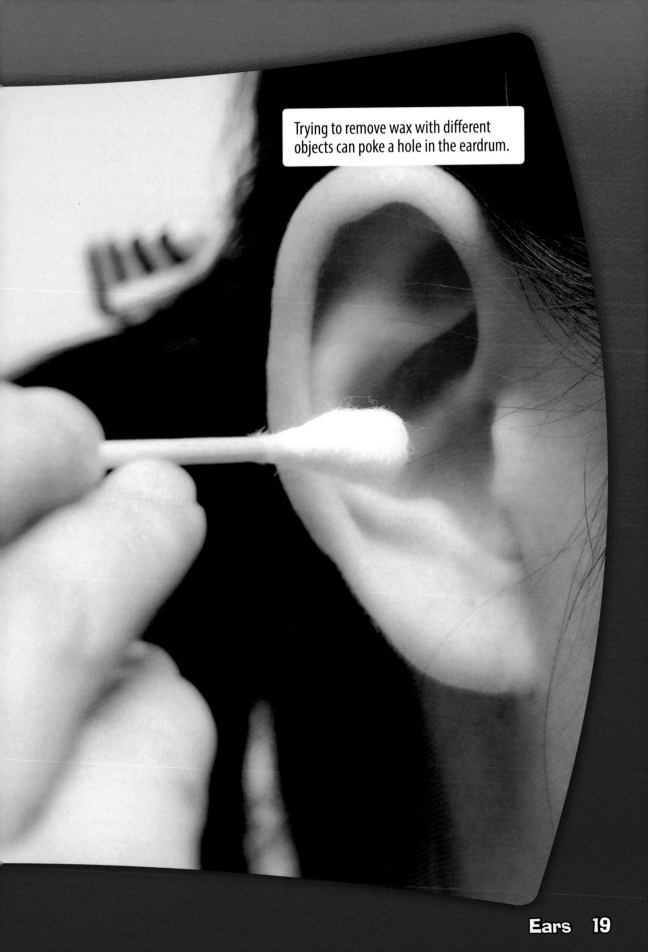

Trying to remove wax with different objects can poke a hole in the eardrum.

Chapter 5
Ear Safety

Your ears never stop working. The ears hear sounds while you sleep, but the brain shuts them out.

There are some ways you can help keep your ears healthy. Most importantly, protect your ears when you are around loud noises, such as the sound of a lawn mower. Earplugs can help protect your ears from sounds that are too loud.

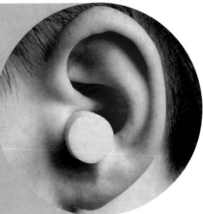

Be gentle with your ears. Protect them when you have a cold by blowing your nose softly. A strong blow can push germs up into your middle ear where they can cause an infection.

Your ears help you stay connected to other people and the world around you. Take care of your ears so you can enjoy your dog's bark and your sister's laugh. Be good to your ears, and they will be good to you.

Quiz

1. **What body system are the ears a part of?**

2. **What happens when sound waves hit the eardrum?**

3. **What are the names of the three tiny bones in the middle ear?**

4. **How do germs cause ear infections?**

5. **What happens when the hairs in the inner ear become bent over?**

6. **Which part of the ear can you see?**

7. **What causes motion sickness?**

8. **Which part of the ear helps you keep your balance?**

9. **What does earwax do?**

10. **Which part of the ear is shaped like a snail shell?**

Key Words

auditory system: the body system that allows us to hear

cochlea: a hollow tube in the inner ear that changes sound waves into messages so the brain can identify a sound

decodes: to change information into something that is easier to understand

eardrum: a thin piece of skin in the ear

germs: very small living things that can make you sick

glands: organs that make natural chemicals in the body

inner ear: the innermost part of the ear

middle ear: the part of the ear between the outer ear and inner ear

outer ear: the fleshy part of the ear you can see

sound waves: waves or series of vibrations in the air

vibrates: to move back and forth very fast

Index

Log on to www.av2books.com

AV² by Weigl brings you media enhanced books that support active learning. Go to www.av2books.com, and enter the special code found on page 2 of this book. You will gain access to enriched and enhanced content that supplements and complements this book. Content includes video, audio, weblinks, quizzes, a slide show, and activities.

AV² Online Navigation

Audio
Listen to sections of the book read aloud.

Book Pages
AV² pages directly correspond to pages in the book.

Video
Watch informative video clips.

Embedded Weblinks
Gain additional information for research.

Key Words
Study vocabulary, and complete a matching word activity.

Try This!
Complete activities and hands-on experiments.

Quizzes
Test your knowledge.

Slide Show
View images and captions, and prepare a presentation.

AV² was built to bridge the gap between print and digital. We encourage you to tell us what you like and what you want to see in the future.

Sign up to be an AV² Ambassador at www.av2books.com/ambassador.

10,00,000